SOMEHOW

ALSO BY BURT KIMMELMAN

Musaics (1992)
First Life (2000)
The Pond at Cape May Point (2002)

*The Poetics of Authorship in the Later Middle Ages: The Emergence
of the Modern Literary Persona* (1996)
The "Winter Mind": William Bronk and American Letters (1998)

SOMEHOW

Poems by Burt Kimmelman

MARSH HAWK PRESS

EAST ROCKAWAY, NEW YORK

2005

FIRST EDITION
05 06 7 6 5 4 3 2 1

Marsh Hawk Press books are published by Poetry Mailing List, Inc., a not-for-profit
corporation under section 501 (c) (3) United States Internal Revenue Code.

Printed in the United States of America by McNaughton & Gunn.

LIBRARY OF CONGRESS CATALOGING-IN-PUBLICATION DATA

Kimmelman, Burt.
Somehow : poems / by Burt Kimmelman. — 1st ed.
p. cm.
ISBN 0-9759197-0-9
1. Fathers and daughters — Poetry. 2. Family — Poetry. 3.
Nature — Poetry. I. Title.
PS3561.I4233S66 2005
811'.54 — dc22
                    2004020972

MARSH HAWK PRESS
P.O. Box 206
East Rockaway, New York 11518-0206
www.marshhawkpress.org

Acknowledgements

Very special thanks to Jane Augustine for her astute editing of these poems, and to Fred Caruso and Claudia Carlson for their artistry in bringing this book to fruition.

Cover art: *Self-Portrait*, an installation of a combined painting and poem first exhibited as part of a show of artist-writer collaborations entitled "Keep Breathing, Keep Shouting," held at the 450 Gallery, New York City, 1996; painting by Fred Caruso; poem by Burt Kimmelman.

Photograph of *Self Portrait*: Joseph Coscia, Jr.

Author photo: Fred Caruso.

Cover and book design: Claudia Carlson.

Many of the poems in this book appeared, often in different forms, in these publications: *Apostrophe, Backwoods Broadsides, College English Notes, Confrontation, Dead Owl, First Intensity, First Life* (Jersey City, NJ: Jensen / Daniels, Publishers, 2000), *House Organ, Mudfish, The Newark Review, ReVisions, The Second Word Thursdays Anthology* (Treadwell, NY: Bright Hill Press, 1999), *Sub Voicive Poetry*, and *The Trumpeter*.

For Diane and Jane

Contents

SOMEHOW

Somehow

Somehow
though the cold
February

a bird
is singing
into the thin

early
light, its trill
then another

among
the branches
empty but for

the red
and blue flecks
incising the

day and
very soon
the riotous

raucous
gangs seizing
territory

so that
in this most
unforgiving

world their
insistence
is all there is.

Sol Lewitt's *Double Pyramid*

Whitney Museum Restaurant, 12.23.00

The other side of
the picture window,
its light borrowed from
above where the stone
blocks at street level

rest adjacent to
a hot dog wagon,
telephone booths and
people on their way
through the winter haze—

we hold whatever
glow there is, the clink
of dishes cutting
across the waves of
conversation, a

reprieve against the
dazzling colors on
the gallery walls.
How incredibly
lucky art is, its

shining like the sun,
undaunted—and we,
too, from below the
summit, in our odd
ways make it come true.

The Evening

Rub your leg
with mine, cricket, scrape
the dark heart and pull

on the night's
heavy gown.

Standing Stones

Calanais, Isle of Lewis, Outer Hebrides

The god commanded a naked stone be set up
and with no marks put upon it. But I had
lost that god or it had become something

like a rain one hears but does not see.
—MICHAEL HELLER

At the top of the hill
the circle of ragged
stones among the moss, peat
and heather, and at its
center the burial
cairn where we fill our hopes
with a glimpse of the sun
here and there—I think of
the great night sky, the moon
without a cloud nearby
and silver picks of stars,
under which the deep silence
was marked by human voice.

The unworked stones standing
tall before the living,
found or quarried, raw and
yet so intelligent
in their perfect array—
how long since they were set—
oddly, they ignore the
aspiration toward grace,
the unforgiving crags

rough to the touch, having
made a space where time, a
mist, can come among us,
and then leave us in tears.

Four Haikus

As the leaves. Descending.
Snow. Lightning. Water.
Wet
leaves
floor
soft
ah
sleep.

* * *

Blackbird, valleys, hills. Hawk
great circles. Redbird,
scarlet
    light
        green
            branching.

* * *

The poem sings also,
but unlike the birds,
what song it might have been.

* * *

Year after year the sun,
squirrels, birds, calling.
Each two trees a gateway.

The Assumption of Matter

The light at least was not to be dismissed.
—WILLIAM BRONK

The newspaper tells us
what we come to know:
"New View of Universe

Shows Sea of Bubbles to Which

Stars Cling." At least until
more accurate sightings
from lensed outposts,

we see the world further from home,
come to feel more and more

our clinging selves
in the perfect stars.

Our galaxies
live
on surfaces

in a cosmos
twenty billion years old. And we peer in

to the emptiness. I
think of your poem
"The Annihilation

of Matter." We

do not
deny, dismiss

the light, Bill,

though we welcome darkness.

The Argument

Something
we left
unsaid? The subway

speeds uptown
on steel wheels. When
will we

see
each other
again? I'll

be home. We'll
have something
to eat. We'll

come to the full
knowledge, your
tongue

in my mouth, one
of us inside
the other.

The Ox Pull

County Fair, Cummington, Massachusetts

The dark snout,
breath in cold air,

taut muscle, sleek skin,

sled of stone—

slide
and smooth the ground under.

The night

probes

not simply for

bruised flesh,
the weight of it. At the end

there is

the turn inward,
what can last—

the brutal struggle

to possess
fire and bear

the beating heart

in hand.

Yellow Flower

Rising up toward
the sunlight the

single yellow
flower holds out

its nectar for
the hummingbird

who comes only
rarely on wings

—its flutter of
air and hookbeak

protruding takes
what it's after.

—Tikal, 2004

Making the Bed

for D.

Summer country. In the morning the leaves
bend

to the window and fold
the house in. Mountains and sun. I fold

the blankets, hand smooth. When
you're here

I know it. The sun crosses

the hand's breadth—

and in your face

the unenterable
image. Under

your eyelids
night unfolds. Pull

the blanket over you
and with it

the darkened air.

Self-Portrait

I lean toward you
as if to say
here I am—not

my eyes or mouth

but this gesture
from the other
side of these words.

The Valentine's Day

The sun fills up the street, the trees, and
the thick air, fat and fresh with the good.
All the birds are coming to the blood

of Spring, the sacrifice
                          cut days in sand.
Warm birds in the withering
                          light, bland
hollow in the heart, stone, pride and food

on the harrowing wing. Find bow, brood
agon done, penance paid in Winter's hand.
All music in our heart's sand, sun's thought

heaving verges of old madness, hunt
dearness, song's wary small loveliness
the slackened foot, eye's nearness; light, our shunt-
ing out heart's hunger, out variedness.
Sure touch of hand, bow in gladness brought.

The Strange Curtain

The runners edge the tree-line along Prospect Park
to the circle at 15th street, or tour the park's
insides, up the wide winding drive. In

the early evening green hills turn bright
and in half-lives gray and then black. Chic

jogging suits or short-cut striped outfits
become dimmer and blend into meadows
and the street beyond. What other comment

could there be, the city muffled in trees
and evening air? Here the young, especially,

make it the distance—sweat and concentration,
repetition, legs, heartbeat, the eyes and mind returning
to the one movement. A dome sky

fits neatly over the boundaries. Runners define
the limits of the park, the sky, themselves.

Later, the night breathes deeply. Above,
the other side of street lamps' strong light signals
a darker history. Our heartbeats range across

a starry terrain we never see, though we know,
we have faith, that beyond the stars there are,

at least, other stars—or else the blackest
fatal sadness we come to, that blank parody.
In the lamplight the body is smooth and toned,

rested now, strong. We make love to stars talking
across a strange curtain. You hold out your hand.

Sidewalk Café, Spring

Sun inside and out
of conversation,

across the walk the
sparrow hopping from

the building's shadow,
we gather in light.

Late October Rain

Water softens
the slight hold of
leaves on branches

bending over
with the weight of
autumn evening—

and the sun next
morning covers
what has fallen.

Gerhard Richter's *Stag*

Museum of Modern Art 3.1.02

The blurred antlers,
obscure eye, taut
musculature—

the flat lines of
forest before,
after—half in

the hunter's sight,
lost in a world
without shadow.

Somewhere

Somewhere
in the dead
cold of winter

a bird
has begun
to sing. O when

does spring
begin its
slowest ascent?

The Fabric

What
we have left

undone, the fabric's
edge, threads

in air. Set up house,
chairs,

window, cover the bed
and table where

we sit—how not see you in

the morning,
any longer remember

the next day, the
next. Yet there

is an end to it—
the light in

the room, unraveled,
moving.

Tales from the Lives of Krsna

A Dog's Life

In a dream
I was newly born. (All the joy,
the thrill of being born!)
And then I realized—
my face
was the face of a dog.
(I panicked.)
With my paws
I tried tugging at my face
—as if it were a mask,
as if I couldn't breathe,
as if it couldn't be true!
It was very sad,
knowing that I was
an infant child.

FIRST LIFE

First Life

for Jane

When you opened
your eyes you smiled

the doctor held
you at arm's length

your cord led back
where you'd never

return.
It took a while

before you cried
then you rested

and sucked. Later
you slept. What had

you seen in that
first instant—light,

movement. Somehow
in your strong voice

we knew it was
you, you who knew

voices—within
the dark, warm world.

The three of us
united

at the moment
of life.

Doisneau's *Ballade pour violoncelle*

But you—how slight—do.

—LOUIS ZUKOFSKY

1.

Little hands
that hold mine—

ten months,
now you'll walk.

2.

Rock

together

in the rocking chair, cool wind
3 A.M.

3.

Above us
the solitary figure,

his instrument,

traversing Brooklyn Bridge.

4.

Photograph
of the real

(Doisneau's
slight metaphor

in the strings).

5.

Listen. There is
the empty street.

6.

Each step

you turn.

Who's there?

Rock

to sleep,

pat my back,
little pats.

7.

The wind, the towering

pylons

and cables

engulf the figure—

8.

as if

we're all alone,

each of us.

In sleep
the clear music

persists.

First Year

Richland, Oregon

O loves of long ago
hello again.
all of us together
with all our other loves and children
twining and knotting
through each other—
intricate, chaotic, done.

—GARY SNYDER

Down "Sparta grade," the valley in sight

hills and mountains not unkind though bare

the gnarled shadows of 4 o'clock, slopes
and gullies, scattered sagebrush, snow on
the distant sky's edges—and below

always the desert, between corn and
alfalfa, flat bottom-land wet from

run-off; this year there's plenty of
water, but there are times when shovels
are used to fight off the "ditch-walker"

who regulates the flow, who turns back
the life force from some desperate farmer.

Before sunset we set out to cross

the near field of hay bales, Jane's birthday,

on her own, slipping on the pebbled
road that runs alongside, and chasing
some quail who strut ahead of us, just

out of reach, and then coming up on
the grass the flurry of shuttled air—

nested starlings, their trajectory
taking them away from us all at
once, wings, flutters, sudden awkward air—

and there are other birds: prairie hens,
jays, owls, robins, hawks, pheasant and grouse.

Here is what consolation there is,

all the old family gone, and we

the new "summer family"—*this* place,
the "home-place," the comfort to be had,
the mountains that are holding us in.

Jane struggles along and it's then that
Diane spots the brown and black smudge, and

adjusting our sight, in the tall grass
the breathing animal stops all three
of us, Jane pointing at what she sees,

the new fawn snuggling against the hay,
settled down deep, legs folded under.

Perhaps we learn by what's familiar,

the similar thing of families,

and in the family of children
one staring blankly at the other,
there's only the scent of the mother,

her call, but then the pull of the world,
its unforgiving complexity;

the breathing slows, standing still, Jane eyes
the deer's two black pools and two large ears
turned toward us to take us in, all three

—yet wait for the mother off somewhere,
the world, beauty, gathering itself.

In the intricate dance, sames and opposites,

it's best to follow "the center line,

with the out-flyers changing—fins, legs,
wings, feathers or fur, they swing and swim
but the snake center fire pushes through. . . ."

This is the first year of our return,
the turn back into soil of what's passed.

7.20.91

For Jane, Age Three

Saying goodnight is saying goodbye—
leave-takings are forever. When
you were born, time began—yet for you
there's no such thing as time.

I drop you off at nursery school,
the colors on the walls, the bright chaos
of finger painting, and cut-out shapes
of trees and people, these two dimensional

worlds without memory, lives lived
at odd angles. In roundabout ways
parents use I tell you we live in a world
of absolutes, the oddnesses not so remote.

For you it's simply instinct, the absence
and return. You pull my hair or let your
head rest in my arm; you ask questions,
questions. The asking, the beauty of talk

is something you've never had to learn.
There are times I say, "I'll always be back."
Strange, since you and I live with such
clarities, that dying has taken its shape.

Saying goodbye seems against all nature.
In this you've shown me the form of love.

Autumn

The cold comes without warning.

Nights, we close the windows—
turn on the lights,

the radio's music—outside
is the world.

Jane does her jigsaw puzzle. Her
small white hands

smooth over the fractures.
In the picture we look on.

No other moment,
we are alive

in the darkened landscape.

Letter to My Dead Brother

I suppose letters to the dead are common.
We need to speak, even when no one's there.
I think of the crazy juxtapositions, the people
and things you loved. Life is a mute grieving.

That's all I can ever say. I have a picture
of you holding Jane at six months, holding
her bottle to her mouth. She used to cry
to herself, a baby when her mother was away.
I'd become afraid. What could I do?

There are objects we inherit from the dead.
They make a strange language we speak
with astonishing clarity—we're surprised by it
yet there it is. The world, its textures, we cherish
them—we cling to them and live out the story.

You never learned how children keep our time.
They don't know us but our words, our faces
shape a world—and we, as if peering out
from behind it, understand how death forms
love, how the photograph becomes memory.

There is a connection that takes the place of
holding one another. I remember you when
Jane puts her arms around my neck. I feel
her warm breath, the blood coursing along.

Waking Up

Jane, you and I in bed
together, the fall
drizzle against the
windows—reds and golds

appear and disappear
in the wind. Like
the weather, we make
our unexpected entrances

and exits. There are
deaths autumn seems
to remember—the trees
bowing down, their

leaves below. My
address book is filling
up with useless
numbers. Never mind—

better not to move. The
floorboards creak if
we get up. Patiently,
Jane places each small

finger, one, another
between my lips.

Flagstones

The flagstones have been uprooted, branches
from underground and leaves scattered
in all directions. Today, after a fierce rain, stones
in the sun turn red and blue—shapes of water

disappearing.

Jane likes to lift the stones, to see the ants and
other strange creatures who burrow for a living. Their
legs, heads, antennae swirl erratically in a panic
of sensing—the loose wires of a civilization coming apart.

We look on.

Finding a Place

Reading the paper on Sunday morning
under lamplight, the white of new snow
filters in along the kitchen's edges.

Silence, although upstairs the thumps and
small voice of my daughter who's fixed a bed
for her doll, and a washing machine,

dining table, adjoining movie
theatre—eventually an entire
village comes to life by putting a chair

in one spot or another, a pillow
under the doll's bedcover, a small
book that's been "written" on a bit of bound

paper, to read before sleep. And after
each careful maneuver, get up and skip
back and forth for a minute or two

thinking what next move, etc. I
hear the water in the tub gurgling. So
it seems this newly made world will be

deluged, swept away—as are all thoughts, all
memories. Someday, I'll drown in my own
juices. But my daughter will be there

in the world building things, and placing them—
taking chances, talking and planning—
finding how to live within winter's light.

Xmas Tally

Jane, Age Six

Sewing Kit

Thread the needle
then push it through

the thick cloth
and pull

Planet Kit

Once the paint dries
hang each globe

from your bedroom ceiling
by a thread

Drawing Kit

Thread the penciled color
across the page

Spell "thread"
Embroider your name

Bedtime

Kiss goodnight
(the thread of your breath).

Late February Sun

Jane, Age Seven

The sunlight startles us awake,
loosens the ground whose shoots and buds—
their traces of red and blue—stand

against the odds. A squirrel makes
for her cache. The first woodpecker
rattles on, wrong yet beautiful—

no sense to the light, how we cleave
to its persistence. This morning
I also make for my cache of

papers, a pile of fallen leaves
on my desk, and instinctively
dig up this past autumn memo

from Jane: "cats birds dogs fish monkeys
whales dolphins." Her hand suddenly
sure and bright—why, though, no snakes?

I praise all creatures, who as if
they had never known winter are
now, too soon, desperately alive.

Getting Ready

Jane, Age Seven

Standing at the sink,
her fingers feel at
the strands of "hair" in
water, add shampoo,

rub and stroke—her smile
of concentration
says she's busy with
important matters—

the small doll getting
ready now to go
out into the world.

These rehearsals, these
evenings, her mother
on the phone, as I
pass the bathroom door

a moment before
nightgown, bed, book, then
covers overhead
to keep out the night.

Jane and Ryan at the Shore

Eight Years of Age

Legs curl under
in the darkened

sand. The waves run
easily up

the beach. Dolphin
fins pace the sea

beyond. Water
has found us all.

—Cape May Point, 1998

Lying in Bed with My Daughter

My half-grown daughter—old enough
to fend around the house—is sick
today, yet finds pleasure in this morning's
television carrying her
past the pain in her stomach. We
lie in bed together—I, in
her nausea, having given up
the day to a nervous leisure.

Slowly the warmth creeps up on us
and we, nodding off together,
forget the noise of busy lives.

Waking My Daughter for School

Jane, Eleven Years Old

I lean over your bed and kiss
your cheek. Everything that might
have happened—a night's tragedy—
has fallen away. Now, in the
moment, we are here together.

Your eyes open. You say "okay"
and sit up, looking around, it seems,
for a dream lost somewhere. You
dress for school, read the back of the
cereal box with your breakfast.

The early daylight overtakes
the kitchen lamp, gathering us.
How routine the day has become—
strange enough, as if it were meant
to be like this. Surely it is.

LATE IN A SLOW TIME

Late January

White sun
across
branches—

windy
day, snow—
no one

believes
the light
will last.

Late February

No denying
the sun, even

in the moment
of cold, crocus

pushing through soil
into the world.

Late March

Streaks of light
cut across

the morning
ice, red buds

along the
simple brush,

a single
bird calling.

Late April

Blossoms then the leaves
among which a trill—
one note, another,
again—alights on
the scattered branches.

Late May

Light against
a bend of
leaves, birds half

in morning's
shadow, slow
heat rising—

several
peeps start up
all at once.

Late June

wave of warblers weaving
chirp to chirp message
—RONALD JOHNSON

The day's signals, each warble,
trill and chirp, on again, off
again, on again, again—

once the red sun has seated
itself below the tree top
creatures cease their back and forth,

a sudden heat gone, slight breeze,
light tendering darkness—one
day, another, another.

Late July

The cicada
winds its plainchant
from earliest

daylight, scattered
like seeds below
the maple tree.

Late August

Warm sun all day
and the chill of

the evening moon—
its full face through

the tops of trees—
the leaves hold on

in the new dark.

Late September

Afternoon sun forcing
shadows under leaves, the
squirrels settle into
busy routines—running

along the limbs of trees,
digging in the warm grass—
already gathering

for the deep interval,
winter far off no more
to be denied in the
chilly dark of evening.

Late October

Red, pink, white
impatiens

growing wild
and tawdry

—half covered
with the fall

of leaves, sun.
No reason

it seems for
the cold air

—the late light
staying on.

Late November

The tree outside
my window is
bare now but for

one brown spot in
the vast slate sky,
a diffidence,

the brittle leaves
holding back what
must come to pass.

Late December

Thin ice along
the fragile branch

bending low of
its own weight, wind

and moon tighten
the new darkness.

BURT KIMMELMAN has previously published three collections of poetry— *Musaics* (1992), *First Life* (2000), and *The Pond at Cape May Point* (2002), a collaboration with the painter Fred Caruso. For over a decade, Kimmelman was Senior Editor of *Poetry New York: A Journal of Poetry and Translation.* He is an associate professor of English at New Jersey Institute of Technology, and the author of two book-length literary-critical studies: *The "Winter Mind": William Bronk and American Letters* (1998) and *The Poetics of Authorship in the Later Middle Ages: The Emergence of the Modern Literary Persona* (1996, paperback 1999). He has also edited *The Facts on File Companion to 20th-Century American Poetry* (2005). He lives in New Jersey with his wife, Diane Simmons, and their daughter Jane.